ENHANCE THE VISION©
Intervention Strategies for Chronic Disrupters

TOOLS TO REGAIN CLASSROOM CONTROL

Diana Day

Credits/Copyright

Contributor
Rick Pehrson

Production Assistant
Wendy Truelove

Cartoons
Chris Barker
Ben Chamley

©1994 Day Publishing & Training
2903 Saturn Road
Garland, TX 75041
Phone (972) 278-7773
Fax (972) 278-8584
www.dianaday.com

ISBN Number: 0-9667646-5-X

Printed in the United States of America

First Printing, July 1994
Second Printing, May 1995
Third Printing, May 1996
Fourth Printing, October 1997
Fifth Printing, July 2001
Sixth Printing, August 2002
Seventh Printing, June 2004
Eighth Printing, September 2004

Table of Contents

Interactive answers on page 45

Chapter 1

ENHANCE YOUR "VISION" TO BECOME MORE POWERFUL & EFFECTIVE

- WHERE DO YOU STAND ON THE MOUNTAIN OF INFLUENCE?

- BECOME THE HIGHLY-RESPECTED PROFESSIONAL YOU'VE ALWAYS WANTED TO BE

- POWERFUL SELF-TALK TO PREVENT BURNOUT & STRESS

©1994 Diana Day Training
www.dianaday.com • 972-287-7773

ESTABLISHING AN EMPOWERED ATTITUDE TO BE MORE POWERFUL & EFFECTIVE

_b_ 1. How many ways can you respond to an acting-out individual?
a) 1   (b) 2   c) 5   d) 10   ~~e)~~ infinite

____ 2. Students are very sensitive to six things. What are they?
a) _facial expression_
b) _tone of voice_
c) _volume of voice_
d) _proximity_
e) _touch_
f) _what you say and your attitude_

_C_ 3. What is the *most* important thing you need to know to be in charge of your students?
(a) How to have good relationships with students
b) To remember that you are the one who's in charge
(c) To know what you expect student(s) to do at all times

_b_ 4. It is better to have one heavy-duty, end-of-the-line consequence rather than several smaller consequences.
a) True   (b) False

_3_ 5. How many voice levels do you use in your classroom (teaching area)? _5_
Name them: _loud, medium, soft_

CREATING AN ORGANIZED, EFFECTIVE CLASSROOM

_d_ 6. Eighty percent of the problems in a classroom result from:
a) Lack of parent support to complete homework
b) Decreased funding for necessary texts or supplies
(c) Overly crowded conditions
d) What's on the desk that should not be there

_4_ 7. Students can use their voices in ____ ways in your classroom.

____ 8. What can you say to the entire classroom to get their attention?
SALAME

____ 9. Where would your classroom procedures fit into your existing rules?
following instructions

____ 10. How would you keep students quiet after written work or a test so the others can finish without distraction?
~~&~~ read a book

©1994 Diana Day Training
www.dianaday.com • 972-287-7773

Its never right do wrong, Its never wrong do right,
Its always right to do right and always wrong to do wrong.

Enhance Your Vision -- Pre/Post Test

IF IT'S NOT HALLOWEEN, DON'T GIVE OUT THE CANDY

____ 11. What are three words that stop arguers and also let them know you're listening?
   I   hear/understand   that ...

_a_ 12. When a student is off-task and you are unable to go to that student, which of the following should you do?
   (a) Redirect from across the room and continue to teach
   b) Stop teaching and threaten to write a referral

____ 13. What's an effective response to a student who tells you, "I don't care"?
   I care enough about you for the both of us
   Yes, you do.

_b_ 14. After you have directed a student to return to his task, you should:
   (a) Wait at his desk for compliance   b) Walk away

_c_ 15. What's the most important aspect of achieving one's goals?
   a) Believing you can do it   (b) Never giving up   c) Writing them down

HOW TO ROLL UP YOUR SLEEVES THE RIGHT WAY

_c_ 16. When a student is not on-task:
   a) Deal with the problem immediately by writing a referral to remove a student
   b) Redirect from across the room loudly, if necessary
   (c) Do what is needed to stop the misbehavior, and discuss the problem with the student later

____ 17. If a student refuses to speak during a problem-solving meeting, what would you say or do?
   pretend they give you the right answer

____ 18. What would you say if a student says that you allowed another student to do something and now you are not letting him/her do it?
   _I understand you want to talk about __ right now we are talking about you._

_c_ 19. When giving a student a direction and the student argues, the maximum times to repeat your direction would be:
   a) Once
   (b) Twice
   c) Three times
   d) Until the student complies

_c_ 20. If a student says, "You're not fair!", you should respond with:
   a) "Life is not always fair."
   b) "Tough!"
   (c) "I understand that you think it's not fair."
   d) In your mind think, "Tough," and say, "Just do it."

Enhance the Vision© - Chapter 1 - EV01
Enhance Your Vision to Become More Powerful & Effective

©1994 Diana Day Training
www.dianaday.com · 972-287-7773

IF IT'S YOUR CLASS, IT'S YOUR PROBLEM

_a_ 21. When should you begin documenting misbehavior?
   (a) After you have redirected and misbehavior continues   b) At the end of the day
   c) After an office referral

___ 22. After how many documentations in one day should a parent contact be made? _2-3_

___ 23. What is the most important reason for keeping detailed, written documentation?
   to CYA, parental support

_b_ 24. How many critical expectations (rules) are there that require an immediate office referral?
   a) three   b) four   c) five   d) six

___ 25. When should you prepare your documentation notebook? _At the beginning of school_

Total your correct answers and multiply by four.
Then, check below to see where you stand on the "Mountain of Influence."
You'll find the answers on page 78.

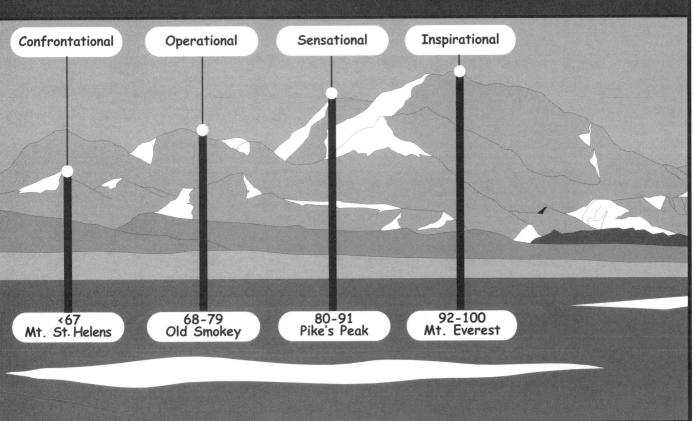

How far have you climbed on the "Mountain of Influence"?

| Confrontational | Operational | Sensational | Inspirational |

| <67 Mt. St. Helens | 68-79 Old Smokey | 80-91 Pike's Peak | 92-100 Mt. Everest |

Enhance the Vision© - Chapter 1 - EV01
Enhance Your Vision to Become More Powerful & Effective

©1994 Diana Day Training
www.dianaday.com • 972-287-7773

Create a Vision of the Teacher You Want to Be

All of us have had people in our lives who pushed our buttons
and were annoying. We know that they manipulate us
to get what they want and we allow it!

Why do some people get what they want from us?

_____

_____

Some reasons that we let someone take advantage of us are because:

1. It might be easier to i _ignore_ the problem than hassling with those who cause the problem.

2. You feel you don't have the sk _ills_ , t _ime_ or e _nergy_ to proactively handle the situation.

Adult and child bullies thrive on people who do not stick up for themselves. Ignoring a problem will rarely make it go away. The problem might stop temporarily, but will begin again, because the bully knows he/she can get away with unacceptable behavior. It is healthy to have an image of how you would handle the most challenging person you know. If you have not been successful to this point, imagine how your ideal person would handle the situation.

Someone/something I need to deal with is:

_____

_____

My Ideal Person(s) to handle this person/problem would be:

_____ .

This person would be strong, confident, speaks his/her mind, warm, caring, tactful, powerful, unafraid and invincible!

Enhance the Vision© - Chapter 1 - EV01
Enhance Your Vision to Become More Powerful & Effective

©1994 Diana Day Training
www.dianaday.com · 972-287-7773

> You are your own inventory of strength.
> Become all that you already are!
>
> Diana Day
> Oklahoma Association of Elementary School Principals Conference, 1995

To intervene in student misbehavior in a confident manner, it's vital to believe in yourself and your good sense and ability to say or do the right thing. You do have the moral fiber to overcome the assault of words, menacing looks and sullen refusal.

Believe In Yourself

(Read this affirmation often to build your self-confidence.)

To Prepare Yourself

I am not going to let this get to me.
I have nothing to fear about this person.
I can handle tough situations.

Think During the Confrontation

I am calm and focused upon a positive outcome.
This person is as upset as I am.
I can control myself.

To Cope in the War of Words & Looks

I am relaxed and remembering to breathe.
I realize I may want to fight, run away or freeze.
I remain objective, repeating what the other person says.
("What you're angry about is that you believe I pick on you?")

To Calm Yourself After the Confrontation

I went over Niagara Falls and lived to tell about it!
I stayed calm with a difficult person.
It will get worked out.
I'm not going to take this home with me. I can and will relax about this.
This problem is a mere grain of sand amid all the beaches in the world.

> "In the quiet of your mind, you can hear your own voice of wisdom."
> Behavior Specialists Conference, Big Island, Hawaii, April 2004 - Diana Day

Check Your Vocabulary at the Door

Many words used in the classroom are outdated and negative to the students who hear them. For over a decade, campuses using *Vision Management*© have successfully introduced new classroom language.

Old Word
Rules

New Word
Classroom Expectations
Recommended expectations are:

1. Be in your assigned seat/area, ready to work when the bell finishes ringing.
2. Have paper, pencils, books and all needed materials every day.
3. HFBO--Keep hands, feet, books and objects to yourself.
4. No profanity, rude gestures, cruel teasing or put downs.
5. Follow the directions of any adult working at this school.

Negative consequences/
Limits

Learning Choices

Students can choose through their behavior where they are going to do their learning:
1. With the class, seated with classmates
2. Away from the other learners, not seated with them but facing the teacher so learning can still continue
3. Not in the classroom

Positive Consequences/
Rewards

Learning Incentives

1. Learning from a unique location
2. Content review in the form of an educational game (*Jeopardy, Concentration,* Baseball game with classroom teams competing--pgs. 28-29)

Time-Out

Refocus Area

1. A place where students can choose to go when they need some private moments to reflect and refocus.
2. A place where the teachers send students who refuse to redirect back to learning and/or are keeping others from doing the same.

Teacher

Educator

Educators need a business card to hand to parents during a conference.

	Working to Serve You Through Education
	YOUR NAME
School Address	Hours
Phone #	School E-Mail

www. Vistaprint.com
250 Cards

Enhance the Vision© - Chapter 1 - EV01
Enhance Your Vision to Become More Powerful & Effective

©1994 Diana Day Training
www.dianaday.com · 972-287-7773

Chapter 2

ESTABLISHING AN EFFECTIVE RESPONSE STYLE

- FOUR VITAL CHARACTERISTICS OF AN IN-CHARGE EDUCATOR

- AVOID FIVE STATEMENTS THAT STRIP YOU OF POWER

- EXPAND YOUR INFLUENCE THROUGH POWERFUL BODY LANGUAGE

Establishing an Effective Response Style

There are __2__ ways an adult can respond when a student acts out. If the adult says and does the __correct thing__, the student will stop misbehaving. However, if the adult says and does the __wrong thing__, the student will continue, or get worse.

Kids are sensitive to:
- f__acial__ e__xpression__
- t__one__ of v__oice__
- v__olume__ of v__oice__
- p__roximity__ of the adult to the student
- t__ouch__
- w__hat__ you s__ay__ (your attitude towards them)

Response Style #1   __I n - C h a r g e__

There are __4__ characteristics of an "In-Charge" teacher.

1. **Know what behaviors you expect at a__ll__ t__imes__.**
- Explain what you expect in d__etail__
- Give a t__ime__ l__imit__ for it to happen.

Write an "In-Charge" direction using the above. ~~expect~~
"__Class__, I __want you to pick-up everything around your desk in one minute so we can__." __go to lunch.__

2. **Communicate f__irmly__ and c__learly__.**
Learn to use "Bear Paws."

B is for "B__ig__ E__yes__." It communicates *"stop-it."*
(Raise eyebrows and do not smile.)

E is for "E__xpectant__ E__yes__. It communicates *"do-it."*
(Raise eyebrows, smile and nod.)

Don't look like this!

The adult can convey many messages with just a "look." If you look directly at a person as you speak, it helps to communicate your sincerity and will increase the intensity of your message. Whatever facial expression you have, the student will m__irror__ you. Your eyes are not meant to overpower the student, but to communicate firmness and caring.

Enhance the Vision© - Chapter 2 - EV02
Establishing an Effective Response Style

©1994 Diana Day Training
www.dianaday.com • 972-287-7773

Eye contact is a cultural variable between age groups or members of the opposite sex.

- If the student looks down, it is considered appropriate for many cultures. Therefore, c_continue_ talking and say, "*Name, nod, if you agree.*"

- If the student turns away and/or puts out a hand towards your face, it would be considered inappropriate, and likely, very rude behavior. Therefore, s_top_ talking for a moment, then say, "*Glance at my eyes. You're good at glancing! (Student often looks away again.) This time when you look at my eyes... keep looking. See if you see any anger. Do you see any? I - am - not - angry. So, continue to look towards me as we speak. Thank you.*"

A is for a_nchor_. The adult must be in close proximity and at eye level to a student when redirecting behavior. Students do not like to be redirected or called down from across the room.

R is for showing and receiving r_espect_. *The adult must sound and act in-charge.*
- N_odding_ communicates your attention and respectful listening.
- It also signals the student subconsciously to respond in a positive fashion.

- Use a power pronoun, such as:
  - I w_ant_
  - I n_eed_
  - I e_xpect_ (used with refusers)
- Voice Levels - Use t_hree_ levels in your classroom
  - Whole class (l_oud_)
  - Table or small group (m_edium_)
  - Individual or private conversation (s____) _low_

P is for p_ause_. When used between words, it communicates, "I - mean - business."

A

W

S

P_ausing_ between words is far better than raising your voice or using sarcasm!

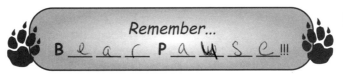
Remember...
B_ear_ P_a_W_S_e!!!

©1994 Diana Day Training
www.dianaday.com • 972-287-7773

3. Provide learning choices (limits) c_onsistently_ when the expectations (rules) are not followed.

THREE **ways to maintain consistency are:**

1) To "walk a p_ath_, looking like you're looking."
Teach from every area of the room--always walking and being obvious in your observations. They need to know you can see everything they do.

2) To drop l_ittle_ b_ombs_, not b_ig_ b_ombs_.
Too often overstated punishments are not doable. Do not threaten and then not follow-through. Choose "little bombs," like sending to a refocus area, that you know you can immediately enforce.
Do not say you will call a parent if you have not checked the file to make sure a correct number is available.

3) Make a list of learning choices that you know you will use consistently--without exception. Explain to your students that these learning choices will occur if they refuse to allow you to teach, or are inconsiderate of others being able to learn.

FIVE **ways to sustain your influence are:**

1) W_alk_ i_nto_ the area of the problem, even if it's the back row/table. Do not redirect from across the room. Lean over the student's desk/table to redirect.

2) When it's time to s_tand_ u_p_ for yourself -- do just that! Stand up! Have an erect posture while facing the student directly. A slouched stance or sitting on the corner of your desk is disempowering.

3) Do not s_it_ to discipline. Call the student to you. Then, you s_tand_ as you redirect the student's activities.

4) S_it_ to counsel; s_tand_ to discipline

5) How to properly touch a student

- Only touch the student's forearm or wrist with t_wo_ fingers. Move them just t_wo_ inches very lightly.
- R_emove_ your hand when the student's chin begins to turn toward you.
- You may also touch with the eraser end of your p_encil_ rather than your fingers. Remember to do this lightly.

4. Deliver p_ositive_ c_omments_ or
l_earning_ i_ncentives_ to get positive results.

You can deliver a comment or incentives in two ways:
1) Intrinsically - gives i_ntrinsic_ encouragement and is long lasting
   Always praise by using the word, "_You_."
   "Rick, (you) thought before (you) got angry. That worked well."
2) Extrinsically - gives m_omentary_ gratification

Response Style #2 N_o_ t_ I_n_ - C_h_a_r_g_e_

The Not-In-Charge Teacher:

1. Tells students what he/she wants after students break the expectations (rules).

2. Tells students they are going to receive punishment for their misdeeds, but fails to follow through. (No action behind his/her words.)

3. Gives students a nagging lecture about their poor behavior, but no real action is taken in the student's eyes.

   When students are mismanaged and do not respond to the *Not-In-Charge* style, the teacher becomes:

   F_____, U_____ and A_____.

Then, the Not-In-Charge Teacher:

1. Lets the problem become intolerable, then slam-dunks with a GIANT consequence.

2. Lashes out in a verbal or physical outburst. Anger is vented but the teacher is likely to feel gui_lty_ about losing self-control.

3. The angry response, with subsequent guilt, leads the teacher to return to be *Not-In-Charge*...whining and begging.

Hence, the cycle continues between being *Not-In-Charge* and *Frustrated-Upset-Angry*.

There are 5 things that teachers say that disempower them:

1. (Why) did you do that? ~~I~~ instead say what happened?
   _____
2. How _____?
3. What _____?
4. Will _____?
5. Will _____? | Find these answers on the next page.

DANGER
RESTRICTED AREA

- **There are two ways an adult can respond when a student acts out:**
    1. Respond correctly and student will stop
    2. Respond incorrectly and student will continue

- **Kids are sensitive to:**
    . Facial expression
    . Tone of voice
    . Volume
    . Proximity
    . Touch
    . What you say (your attitude towards them)

"Repetition is the mother of all skills."

- **There are four characteristics of an In-Charge teacher:**
    1. Know what behaviors you expect at all times
        a. Explain in detail what you expect
        b. Give a time limit for completion
    2. Communicate firmly & clearly
    3. Provide learning choices consistently when expectations are not followed
    4. Deliver positive comments or learning incentives to get positive results

- **There are five things that teachers say that disempower them:**
    1. They ask: "Why did you...." Never ask a "why" question!
        Ask: "What's happening?" Or "What happened?"
    2. How many times do I have to tell you?
    3. What am I going to do with you?
    4. Will you...? O.K.?
    5. Will you try to... Say, "Does that mean, yes, you are going to or, no, you are not?"

JUST SAY "YES!"

- **Use the "YES Technique" when responding to students who are upset.** Always repeat what they've said so they will respond with a "yes." Do this because:
    1. They will know you are listening.
    2. When listened to, they will calm down.
    3. They will, therefore, be more likely to listen to you.

Example	
E	TEA: "Dan, let's get your work started."
x	STU: "I hate this stuff."
a	TEA: "You hate it?"
m	STU: "Uh huh."
p	TEA: "What's happening that you hate it so much?"
l	STU: "It's too hard."
e	TEA: "Has it always been too hard?"
	STU: "Uh huh."
	TEA: "Let me show you an easy way to do it."

16

Chapter 3

MAPS--Don't Leave Home Without Them

"STUDENTS, I WANT YOU TO TAKE YOUR SEATS!"

- DECREASE PROBLEMS USING "MAPS"--
  GUIDE STUDENTS TO PROPER BEHAVIOR

- QUICKLY AND EFFECTIVELY TEACH ROUTINES & PROCEDURES

- PREVENT MISBEHAVIOR WITH PROACTIVE ORGANIZATION &
  COMMUNICATION

©1994 Diana Day Training
www.dianaday.com · 972-287-7773

MAPS

In one day, a class repeats routines time and again.
To reduce your wear-and-tear continuously repeating instructions,
create a "routine or procedure" for *all* of your repetitious directions.

AN EASY & SUCCESSFUL WAY TO DO THIS IS BY TEACHING:

M _____

A _____

P _____

S _____

1. No talking to each other
2. Raise hand + wait to be called on
3. Whisper voice
4. Blended voice

A blended voice is when you can't hear o____ v_____
a_____ a_____ in the group.

Determine your routines by creating specific directions that you will use each
time during a specific task. These specific directions will tell the students:

- What m_aterials_____ they need or do not need on t_heir__ d_esk___.
- To always have a c_an___-d_o_attitude.
- Where to place themselves d_uring_____ the a_____.
- How to s_peak_____ or a_nswer_____ to the teacher or other students.

Where do MAPS fit into your plan?
following directions
_____

ONE AT A TIME!   NO TALKING!

Enhance the Vision© - Chapter 3 - EV03
MAPS--Don't Leave Home Without Them

Teaching A Lesson/Lecture Format

M _clear desk of everything but needed supplies_

A _can do!_

P _stay in assigned seat_

S _raise hand & wait for permission to speak_

Small Group Work (3 or more)

M _Bring needed supplies_

A _can do!_

P _stay in assigned area_

S _blended voices_

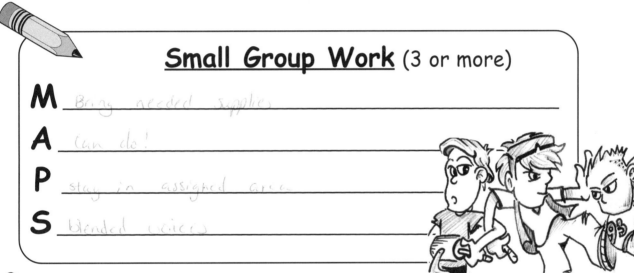

Cooperative Partners (2 students)

M _clear desk of everything but needed supplies_

A _Can do!_

P _Stay in assigned seat_

S _Whisper voices_

19

MAPS

Take 30 Seconds & Make Your Day!

Transition

STATIC	MOVING
M _put away and get_	**M** Same _____
P _Stay_ in _assigned_ seat	**P** When _walking_
S No _talking_	**+**
	S No _talking_

Discussion

M Clear desk of everything but paper & pencil for n_ote_ -t_aking_ only.

A _Can do_

P S_tay_ in a_ssigned_ seat.

S Raise h_and_ and w_ait_. Stay on t_opic_.

Taking A Test

library book

M Put free time activity under your s_eat_. Clear desk of everything but needed s_____.

A _can do_

P S_tay_ in a _ssigned seats_ seat.

S No t_alking_ to each other. Signal for h_elp_.

Enhance the Vision© - Chapter 3 - EV03
MAPS--Don't Leave Home Without Them

©1994 Diana Day Training
www.dianaday.com • 972-287-7773

Entering The Classroom

1. _Walk_____

2. Put s_upplies_____on desk - Sharpen Pencil, if needed

3. Begin R_eady_____-to-W_ork_____ Box

4. C_lassroom_____ V_oices_____

Temporarily Exiting Classroom

Individual Class	All Classes In Hall
M S_ecure___ s_upplies___	**M** S_ecure____ s_upplies__
P S_ingle_____ file	**P** D_ouble_____ file
S No talking	**S** _Classroom voices_____

Individual Seat Work

M _put library book under your seat_____
_Clear desk of everything_____

A _Can do!_____

P _Stay in seat_____

S _No talking - signal for help_____

Enhance the Vision© - Chapter 3 - EV03
MAPS--Don't Leave Home Without Them

©1994 Diana Day Training
www.dianaday.com • 972-287-7773

MAPS for Outside the Classroom

HALLWAY

- Walk on the right side and go directly to class
- Walk; no running
- Keep HFBO to self
- Leave no personal trash on the floor
- Classroom voices; no yelling

Call this the "PASS"
"Patient And Silent Steps"

REST ROOM

- Use facilities as intended and keep them clean
- Keep HFBO to self
- Wash hands; put trash in cans
- No playing or staying
- Classroom voices; no yelling

Call this the "MYOBZ"
"Mind Your Own Business Zone"

CAFETERIA

- Enter at the back of the line; no cutting
- Treat the cafeteria workers with courtesy
- Keep HFBO to self
- Stay in your seat until dismissed
- Classroom voices; no yelling
- Clean up your area (including floor)
- Follow the directions of any adult

Call this the "FCFTB"
"Food Court for the Brain"

YARD/CAMPUS

- Stay in assigned area only
- Share equipment
- HFO to self
- No teasing, bullying, fighting or poor sportsmanship
- Immediately follow directions of adult(s) on duty

Call this the "BLAST"
"Be Like Angels Standing Together"

ASSEMBLIES

- Leave all backpack/supplies in locker/classroom
- Line up on signal to enter or exit
- Stay in your original seat
- Keep HFBO to self
- Show appreciation by not talking or calling out; give applause when appropriate

Call this the "GIFT"
"Gathering In Familiar Territory"

LIBRARY

- Handle all materials/equipment with care
- Keep HFBO to self
- Stay on task
- No talking unless instructed to do so

Call this the "WORM"
"Where Our Reading Multiplies"

Enhance the Vision© - Chapter 3 - EV03
MAPS--Don't Leave Home Without Them

©1994 Diana Day Training
www.dianaday.com · 972-287-7773

MAPS

When teaching procedures,
it is easy to over-direct by using *too many directions*.
It can become confusing and too long for students to listen.
One solution is the following script. The directions become
a formula and are consistent each time. Once the script
is learned, it can be substantially shortened.

MAPS Script

"<u>Eyes on Me</u> (or Look at Me).

We are about to (<u>Name the MAP-eg...'have a discussion about...'</u>)

<u>I want</u> you to <u>follow my directions</u>:

<u>When I give you the signal</u>, <u>I want</u> you to (<u>List Materials</u>).

> *Check for Comprehension with Off-Task Students*
> *"Todd, tell us one supply you will need."*
> *If incorrect: "Todd, keep listening. I'm coming back to you.*
> *Who knows what materials we need to have ready? (Wait.) Correct.*
> *Todd, what is one supply? Correct! I knew you knew it!"*

M Materials

Everyone, please take out your materials. (Give Signal + Expectant Eyes)
Materials are ready, students. Great! (Walk a Path + "Look Like You're Looking")

A Attitude

Your brain believes what you tell it.
What attitude will you have? (<u>Can Do!</u>)

P Placement

There are two more things I need you t o do:
I need you to (<u>stay in your assigned group</u>).

          and

S Speak

to speak, or to answer a question, use (<u>raise hand and wait</u>).

> *Check for Comprehension of Students who "Often Forget"*
> *"(<u>Name</u>), will you be in or out of your seat?*
> *(<u>Name</u>), will you be raising your hand or calling out?"*

Any questions?"

Enhance the Vision© - Chapter 3 - EV03
MAPS--Don't Leave Home Without Them

©1994 Diana Day Training
www.dianaday.com • 972-287-7773

MAPS

What are reasons a teacher should use MAPS?

_____

_____

How will I teach my students MAPS?

WHAT SUPPLIES WILL I NEED?

HOW WILL I INTRODUCE THE TOPIC OF "MAPS"?

IF I MODEL HOW TO USE MAPS, WHAT WILL I DO?

I WILL NEED THEM TO ROLE-PLAY A MAP. HOW WILL I DO THIS?

WHEN WILL I DO THIS?

Remember!
The MAPS script is a uniform method to teach any instructional procedure to your students. When you are introducing the concept of MAPS, the script in this book is in its longest, most complete form. Using this script, or a shortened version consistently, will help the class understand that when you ask them to transition, work independently, or form small groups, it is to be accomplished the same way each time. Each routine will become a standard procedure. You can shorten your "MAPS script" as your students become proficient at your routine requests.

Eventually, you'll give them a direction, and they will respond without delay or behavior problems.

HOW WILL I DISPLAY MY MAPS?

WHAT WILL HELP ME TO REMEMBER TO USE THEM?

CAN I CREATE ICONS INSTEAD OF ACTUAL WORDS?
WHAT WOULD MY SYMBOLS BE?

"I'll take Mystery Meats for $100."

Chapter 4

If It's Not Halloween, Don't Give Out the Candy

- Four Ways to Use Intrinsic Verbal Motivation

- Ten Exciting, FREE Celebrations

- Teach Students to Self-Assess in Order to Self-Manage

Affirming Gestures/Celebrations

Here's an alternative to stickers, stars, stamps and food rewards. It's something that won't cost a cent and has lasting effects. And, it's fun! Students can choose which celebrating gesture they give to one another, or the teacher can choose which is appropriate.

VISION MANAGEMENT© CELEBRATIONS

1.

2.

3.

4.

5.

6.

7.

8.

9.

10.

Find these answers on page 78.

Elementary students readily enjoy this activity.

Middle school students certainly need affirmation, but most are shy and reluctant to enjoy this activity. They do not want to look foolish in front of their peers. If middle school teachers are enthusiastic and fun-loving, it encourages similar behavior in their students.

Some secondary teachers have:

1. Demonstrated a few of the gestures and had teams of four to six students create new ones they would rather use.
2. Created a spinner with the gestures around the circumference. Students received the gesture they landed upon.

WHAT IDEA DO YOU HAVE THAT WILL MAKE THIS WORK FOR YOU?

_____

_____

Enhance the Vision© - Chapter 4 - EV04
If It's Not Halloween, Don't Give Out the Candy

©1994 Diana Day Training
www.dianaday.com · 972-287-7773

Academic Baseball Review

WHEN TO USE ACADEMIC BASEBALL

When a review is needed, it often seems the only person answering the questions is the teacher! A great learning incentive for positive behavior is to challenge the students to a game of baseball. If the students have shown cooperation, they have earned the special review.

GETTING READY TO PLAY

The day before the review, give students index cards on which to write questions (with answers) that they believe will be on an exam. On the day of the review, draw a baseball diamond on the chalkboard or create an overlay using page 29. Divide the class into two teams and flip a coin to see which team "bats" (answers) first. Set the timer for a specified period of time or play for a specified number of innings.

Each team selects a batting order and sits on one side of the room. To add movement, set up four chairs in a diamond shape as bases with the one closest to the front of the room being home. If movement is not desired or practical, the teacher can keep score on the board or overhead.

RULES OF THE GAME

* The team winning the coin toss chooses to bat (answer questions) first or let the other team bat first.
* The game begins as the first batter **walks** up to the "home" chair.
* Using the students' index cards, ask each team member in turn a question.
* If the batter answers correctly, he/she **walks** to the "first base" chair.
* If wrong, the batter is out and goes to the end of the batting order line.
* If a player answers out of turn or misbehaves, the team receives an out.

HOME RUN OPTION

The teacher can prepare home run cards with "tougher" questions. A batter may request to go for a home run. If answered correctly, the student gets a home run. If the student's answer is incorrect, a double play is recorded with the batter and the most advanced runner being declared out.

The inning proceeds using regular baseball rules until three outs are made. The score is recorded and the other team comes to bat.

IN CASE OF A TIE

Play can be extended into extra innings with the team leading at the end of a complete extra inning being the winner.

Or, an optional "toss-up" teacher question can be asked with anyone from either team being able to answer. The first correct answer is credited with a home run and wins.

Enhance the Vision© - Chapter 4 - EV04
If It's Not Halloween, Don't Give Out the Candy

©1994 Diana Day Training
www.dianaday.com • 972-287-7773

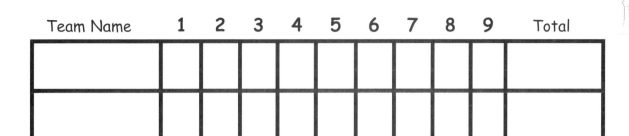

Team Name	1	2	3	4	5	6	7	8	9	Total

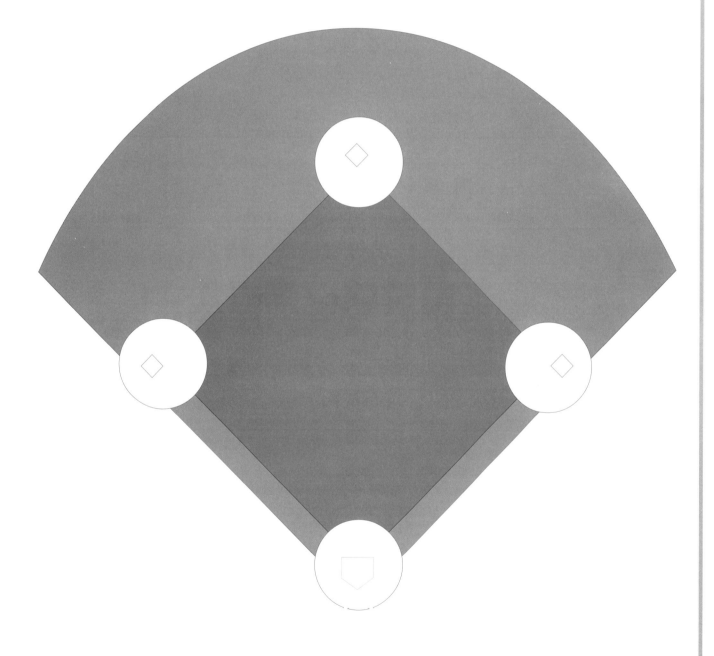

©1994 Diana Day Training
www.dianaday.com • 972-287-7773

Here are two examples of ways to
build intrinsic motivation.

Ima Restin	
Name	
Congratulations *You did it!*	

WANT TO ...
UP YOUR GRADE?

Do you have sluggish learners? To motivate performance, tell your students you will give them a card with 10 boxes. They are to write their name in ink on the top of the card.

Whenever they make a grade of "C" or better, you will rubber stamp one box on the card. When the card is filled, it allows them to raise their lowest grade by one level.

PERSONALIZED STUDENT-MADE
STATIONARY

Mr. Yowza
Science Teacher

Do you want written communication to be noticed by your parents? Create a great home-school public relations builder.

Allow your students to draw a picture of you...without getting in trouble! Have a contest where other teachers choose the drawing that represents you the best. Your correspondence has the student-made drawing in the corner. Credit is given to the artist at the bottom of the page.

Every year have another contest. Frame each year's winning picture asking the student to sign and date it. Display these in your classroom.

Artist: Michael Angelo-6th grade

Teaching Intrinsic Motivation

Students do not always need extrinsic incentives to follow directions or to do what is required of them. If used *with moderation*, extrinsic incentives can be fun and motivational. Too much extrinsic motivation, creates a child who will only work for "things," and will not learn to be self-motivated or self-managed.

Intrinsic Verbal Motivation is Vital to:

- G_____ students on-t_____
- K_____ students on-t_____

Four types of intrinsic, verbal motivation:

1 dba _____

2 Larry, Moe & Curley

3 Move It or Lose It!

4 Delayed Approval

©1994 Diana Day Training
www.dianaday.com • 972-287-7773

1 dba, Desired Behavior Acknowledgement

It's Important Because:

The teacher focuses on the students who p_____ the task. These students are usually i_____.

It allows students not performing the task to h_____ the direction again in a p_____ format.

It creates a p_____ c_____ in the classroom rather than a teacher pointing out everyone who is off-task.

WHEN USING dba:

· **Give a specific direction.**
   "Put your microscopes in the cabinet and stack your lab reports in the center of your table."

· **Find someone performing the task.**

· **Say the student's name and the specific direction being followed.**
   "Table one has their microscopes in the cabinet."

More examples:
"Table four has stacked their lab reports."

"Tables two and three have both their microscopes in the cabinets and lab reports stacked in the middle of their table."

Write a specific direction appropriate for your grade level.

Direction: _____

_____

Acknowledge someone or a group doing it correctly.

Use dba: _____

_____

Enhance the Vision© - Chapter 4 - EV04
If It's Not Halloween, Don't Give Out the Candy

©1994 Diana Day Training
www.dianaday.com • 972-287-7773

2 Larry, Moe & Curley

The name will help you remember this verbal motivation!

- Give a specific direction. After using "dba" motivation, you may see a student still not performing the task.

- Move to the area of the off-task student. **Praise a student to the right and left of the student who is not on-task.** ("Larry and Curley have finished their tests and have put them in the proper place.")

- When the non-performer performs the task, comment, in a <u>matter-of-fact way</u>, about what he/she has done. ("Moe has his test face down waiting for further direction.")

  If the student does not perform the task, anchor and say, "Moe, I expect (<u>give specific direction</u>) by the time I start the lesson."

  Use your discipline plan if the student continues to refuse.

Remember, always give "Moe" praise!!!

Enhance the Vision© - Chapter 4 - EV04
If It's Not Halloween, Don't Give Out the Candy

©1994 Diana Day Training
www.dianaday.com • 972-287-7773

3 Move It or Lose It!

If you are someone who parks yourself on a stool or chair for your career, you may end up with:

- an unruly class
- a wide bottom
- *or both!*

CAUTION

WIDE LOAD

One of the best ways to get and keep students on-task, is to circulate everywhere to be sure that they do what you've requested. Sometimes just a smile, as you walk in their direction, is enough to get students who sit in the back of the room to participate. While cruising around the room, it is important to **STOP** at students' desks to praise their effort or to ask if you can be of assistance to them.

Have you finished your *SEAT* work?

C. BARKER © 1994

A good teacher is like a shark...ALERT & ALWAYS MOVING!

34

4 Delayed Approval

There will be times when you are unable to move about the room because you are leading an experiment or guiding a group through an activity. Keep an index card in your pocket or waistband and wear a neck pen to make notes of students who are doing a particularly fine job. After you have transitioned into the next activity, and have the attention of the entire class, read from your card the students who were doing a good job. Be specific with your comments! Inject humor, if possible.

"You are great! No jest!"

Example:

"Sara is the first name I wrote on my card. She may need oxygen before we begin our discussion. While doing her independent study, she NEVER CAME UP FOR AIR! Great concentration, Sara!"

You can consider yourself to be a GOOD teacher when you can get superior work from average students.
- Mom Betty Weber

I can live for two months on a good compliment.
- Mark Twain

Wear a smile & have friends;
wear a scowl & have wrinkles.
What do we live for if not to make the world less difficult for our students?
- George Eliot

35

©1994 Diana Day Training
www.dianaday.com • 972-287-7773

PACE FORM

Planned Action & Commitment Everyday

WINNER AND STILL CHAMPION

Name _____
Date _____

My Goal _____

Specific Action Steps	Monday	Tuesday	Wednesday	Thursday	Friday	Daily Average
1.						<u>CALCULATE YOUR DAILY AVERAGE.</u> Place each daily total here: Monday ____ Tuesday ____ Wednesday ____ Thursday ____ Friday ____ * Add each day <u>Total</u> ____ * Divide the total by 5. This is your daily average: ____ See the Self-Scoring Key for your results.
2.						
3.						
4.						
My Daily Total						

Evaluating My Action Steps
- 5 = I did my very best today.
- 4 = I really came close to doing my best.
- 3 = I could have done better.
- 2 = I could have done a lot better.
- 1 = I didn't do very well today.

Self-Scoring Key   **My Daily Total**
- 18-20 = I did my very best today.
- 16-18 = I really came close to doing my best.
- 13-15 = I could have done better.
- 10-12 = I could have done a lot better.
- Under 9 = Are my action steps realistic?

Chapter 5

SIX WAYS TO ROLL UP YOUR SLEEVES THE RIGHT WAY

- WHAT TO DO WHEN YOU DO EVERYTHING RIGHT AND THINGS STILL GO WRONG

- WORD-FOR-WORD SCRIPTS TO FIT EVERY SCENARIO

- FIVE BEST ANSWERS TO STOP BACK TALK

©1994 Diana Day Training
www.dianaday.com • 972-287-7773

MANAGING "PIVOTAL" STUDENTS

A "pivotal" student is one who typically models the antics of far more challenging students. Since "pivotals" are capable and willing to be cooperative when managed appropriately, it is important to employ a more direct manner of management with them. These students need to be told, kindly but firmly, *exactly what is expected of them* to accomplish their academic or behavior goals.

Pivotal students do not have the challenging psychological drives of more difficult students. They are followers. That is why they comply more readily. They will usually become compliant if the teacher will confront them with immediate, direct intervention.

REMEMBER! DO NOT USE AN AUTHORITARIAN OR PARENTAL MANAGEMENT STYLE OF COMMUNICATION. YOUR GOAL IS TO SEEK COOPERATION, NOT TO WIN A VERBAL BATTLE.

WHO'S A REFUSER?

When a student refuses to perform appropriately using positive prevention (MAPS, DBA, Anchoring, etc.), the next step is to employ stronger intervention. **A r_efuser_ is someone who knows what to do and is capable of doing the task but will not do it.**

These students are testing your fortitude to encourage them to do it. Others are saying, "My will is greater than your will. I CAN outlast you!"

Either way, it is imperative that you do not personalize this student's refusal as purely directed at you. This student is modeling the antics of a more challenging student, and will often comply if the appropriate disciplinary interventions are used.

Your **5** Word Answer to Arguers

The "IF I ... GAME"

(Manipulation)

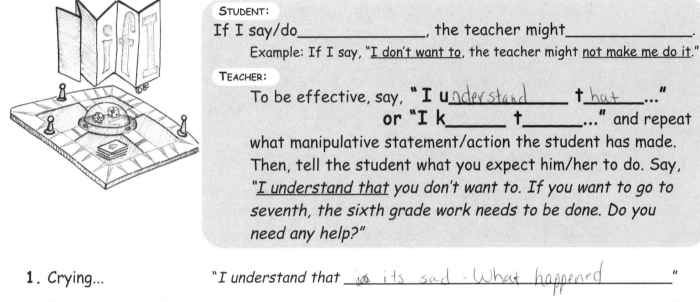

STUDENT:
If I say/do_____, the teacher might_____.
Example: If I say, "<u>I don't want to</u>, the teacher might <u>not make me do it</u>."

TEACHER:
To be effective, say, "**I u**<u>nderstand</u> **t**<u>hat</u>..."
or "**I k**_____ **t**_____..." and repeat
what manipulative statement/action the student has made.
Then, tell the student what you expect him/her to do. Say,
"<u>I understand that</u> you don't want to. If you want to go to
seventh, the sixth grade work needs to be done. Do you
need any help?"

1. Crying...   "I understand that <u>is its sad · What happened</u>"

2. "This is stupid..."   "I understand that _____"

3. "I hate this stuff..."   "I understand that _____"

4. "You're mean..."   "I understand that <u>you think I'm mean</u>"

5. "That's not fair..."   "I understand that <u>you think its not fair</u>"

6. "The other kids were doing it, too..." "I understand that <u>you want to talk about</u>
<u>right now we are talking</u>"
<u>about you.</u>

"If I...Game" Activity

A direction you might give one of your challenging students_____
_____

What might be the student's "If I Game..." (manipulative answer)?

If I (student says/does) _____

the teacher might _____

What would you answer?_____
_____

Enhance the Vision© - Chapter 5 - EV05
Six Ways to Roll Up Your Sleeves the Right Way

©1994 Diana Day Training
www.dianaday.com • 972-287-7773

Managing Refusers When You Have No Time

Are there days when you have more lesson than you have time? That's precisely when a "refuser" robs you of the precious time remaining by distracting others from their task.

To get back on track *quickly,* you might not want to use the technique on page 39. Use this instead. Continue to teach as you move to the area where the refuser is located. Anchor quickly at the refuser's work area, and say the following:

> **"(<u>Name</u>), I need you to (<u>give specific direction</u>)."**

If the student argues, or plays the "If I … Game."
   "She did it to me first."
   (The student is thinking: If I say, "She did it first," the teacher
                                        might leave me and go to her.)

You repeat:
> **"(<u>Name</u>), I need you to (<u>give specific direction</u>)."**

If the student argues, or again plays the "If I … Game," say the following:
> **"(<u>Name</u>),** (pause, giving Big Eyes) **I need you to** (pause)
> **(<u>give specific direction</u>). Thank you."** (Walk away.)

THERE ARE ONLY 2 THINGS THIS STUDENT CAN DO:
   1. Follow your direction
   2. Not follow your direction

Continue to teach. If the student does not follow your direction within the ample time you have given, your behavior management plan goes into effect. Apply a learning choice.

EXPECT SUCCESS

The "When-You-Have-No-Time" Activity
What is something one of your more challenging students might do when you feel you have no time to manage the disruptions?

WHAT WOULD YOU ANCHOR AND SAY?	EXAMPLES:
1. _____	"Rob, stop talking. Finish your work."
2. _____	"Rob, stop talking. Finish your work."
3. _____	"Rob, (pause, giving Big Eyes) stop talking. (pause) Finish your work."
4. _____	Walk away. Give time for redirection to occur.
5. _____	"Do you not care about your work? Please move to the Refocus Area. We'll talk about this later."

Enhance the Vision© - Chapter 5 - EV05
Six Ways to Roll Up Your Sleeves the Right Way

©1994 Diana Day Training
www.dianaday.com • 972-287-7773

How to Manage a Disruption

Use this technique when the student does not respond to positive prevention (MAPS) and does not perform the task as required.

Situation #1: You are unable to go to the student.

ACTION: 1. **Speak matter-of-factly.**

"Name, please (take out your book). Thank you." (Big eyes & nodding)

2. **Continue to teach. Do not stop to wait for compliance.**
A p_ivotal_ will obey. A more c_hallenging_ student will attempt a confrontation if the class focuses on his disobedience.

Situation #2: You are able to go to the student, or the student continues to refuse.

ACTION: 1. **Build a Bridge**
Direct other students to an i_ndependent_ a_ctivity_.

"Class, please (read the rest of the page finding the longest river and and three major cities on it)."

2. **Divide and Conquer**
Reinforce students around the p_roblem_ s_tudent_.

Walk to students sitting around the problem student. Smile, privately directing them to work. Do not look or speak to the refusing student.

3. **Be an Eagle**
Land at the r_efuser's_ d_esk_.

Anchor at the refuser's desk.
*"(Name), the direction was to (take out your book).
I want (need or expect) you to (take out your book)."*

Situation #3: If the student continues to refuse...

Action: 1. **Be calm and unemotional.**
Bend over and quietly speak to the student.

*"(Name), if you do not (take out your book), you will need to move away from the learners.
Think - about - it, (Name).
I want you to be successful."*

2. **Walk away.**
Do not wait for compliance.

3. **Follow your behavior management plan for continued refusal.**

Enhance the Vision© - Chapter 5 - EV05
Six Ways to Roll Up Your Sleeves the Right Way

©1994 Diana Day Training
www.dianaday.com • 972-287-7773

A One-Minute Talk with a Refuser

This works because it shows the student you will not back down. You are not intimidated by his/her refusal behaviors in your class. Usually this student is not as disrespectful in private since classmates are not there to support misbehavior.

Calm & Private
THE "LATER TALK"

"(Name), thank you for leaving your (math class).

I appreciate it. (pause)

(Name), I'm really concerned about you. (nod, then pause)

Today in class, I asked you to (tell the direction given)

and you (tell what student did). I - can't - allow - you - to - continue - to (tell what student did).

For Elementary: When you return to class, it's important that you follow my directions. When I ask you to (_____), then what will you do?

For Secondary: Tomorrow when you return to class, it's important that you follow my directions and (name desired behavior). When I ask you to (_____), then what will you do?

(Name), thank you. I'll look forward to your cooperation when you return to class." (Smile and nod.)

Enhance the Vision© - Chapter 5 - EV05
Six Ways to Roll Up Your Sleeves the Right Way

©1994 Diana Day Training
www.dianaday.com • 972-287-7773

YOUR "LATER TALK"

This script will become one of your most valuable tools. Many misbehaving students believe that once they exit your room, whatever disrespect or lack of cooperation afforded you, is now cancelled out because they are no longer there. Continuous mistreatment of you might occur day after day.

During your prep/conference/team time, ask permission from the offending student's teacher to speak to the student in the hall for just 60 seconds. This can make a **powerful impact!** Think, would you be willing to take 60 seconds from non-instructional time to save hours of squabbling during your instructional time?

Send your students the message that you and your colleagues can find them anywhere to straighten out problems. *This is a kind but firm conversation.*

Create your personalized "Later Talk" below:

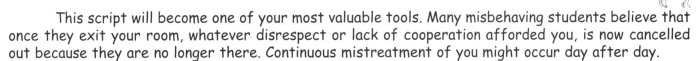

Calm & Private

THE "LATER TALK"

Enhance the Vision© - Chapter 5 - EV05
Six Ways to Roll Up Your Sleeves the Right Way

©1994 Diana Day Training
www.dianaday.com • 972-287-7773

IMPORTANCE OF SELF-CONTROL

When a teacher checks for understanding, some students will answer in an overt (in your face) or covert (silent treatment, rolling of eyes) manner. This display of disrespect lowers your threshold of patience. Many students' motivation is to upset you and have you lose emotional control.

It is essential NOT to lose control when giving directions or instruction. If the student loses control, he/she goes to the office. **If you lose control, you can lose your job.** You must always consider what you jeopardize when you are anything but professional.

TEACHER RESPONSE TO BACK TALK:

Student back talk/action -- Teacher response

1. **I** <u>Don't know</u> -- <u>I do know and give correct answer</u>

2. **Opposite** <u>answer</u> -- <u>No and give correct answer</u>

3. **Refusal** <u>to speak</u> -- <u>That's right and give correct answer</u>

4. **I** <u>don't care</u> -- <u>I care enough about you for the both of us</u>

5. **Personal** <u>insult or racial slur</u> -- a). T<u>emporarily ignore</u>
   b). G<u>ive correct answer</u>
   c). D<u>eal w/ slur/remark at end</u>

C. BARKER © 1994

O.K. KIDS, PUT A LID ON IT !!!

PAGE ANSWERS

8 ignore, skills, time, energy

12 2, correct thing, wrong thing, facial expressions, tone voice, volume voice, proximity, touch, what, say, In-Charge, 4, all times, detail, time limit, firmly, calmly, Big Eyes, Expectant Eyes, mirror

13 continue, stop, anchor, respect, Nodding, want, need, expect, 3, loud, medium, soft, pause, Bear Pause

14 consistently, path, little bombs, big bombs, Walk into, stand up, sit, stand, Sit, stand, two, two, remove, pencil

15 positive comments, learning incentives, internal, you, momentary, Not In-Charge, Frustrated, Upset, Angry, guilty

18 Materials, Attitude, Placement in Class, Speaking Voice, 1. No talking, signal for help. 2. Raise hand and wait for permission to speak. 3. Whisper voices 4. Classroom or blended voices one voice above another's, materials, their desk, can do, during activity, speak, answer

19 Top M=Clear desk of everything but "needed" supplies-- A=Can do!-- P=Stay in assigned seat-- S=Raise hand and wait for permission to speak

19 Mid M=Bring/take "needed" supplies/equipment-- A=can do! P=Stay in assigned area/with assigned group-- S=Blended voices

19 Btm M=Put free time activity under seat. Clear desk of everything but "needed" supplies-- A=can do!-- P=Stay in assigned seat-- S=Whisper voices

20 Top (Static) M=Put away and get (out)...-- P=Stay in assigned seat-- S=No talking (Moving) M=Put away and get-- P+S=When walking No talking

20 Mid M=note-taking-- A=can do!-- P=Stay in assigned seat-- S=hand, wait, topic

20 Btm M=seat, supplies-- A=can do!-- P=Stay, assigned-- S=talking, help

21 Top 1. Walk-- 2. supplies-- 3. Ready, Work-- 4. Classroom voices

21 Mid (Individual Class) M=Secure Supplies-- P=Single (All classes) M=Secure supplies-- P=Double file-- S=Classroom voices

21 Btm M=Put free time activity under desk. Clear desk of everything but needed supplies. A=can do!-- P=Stay in seat-- S=No talking to each other-signal for help

31 Get, task, Keep, task, desired behavior acknowledgement

32 performs, ignored, hear, positive, positive, climate

38 refuser

39 understand that, know that, 1. it's sad, but I need... 2. you think this is stupid, but... 3. this may not be your favorite thing to do, but... 4. you think I'm mean, but... 5. you think it's not fair, but... 6. you want to talk about other students, but we're not talking about them...

41 pivotal, Challenging, independent activity, problem student, refuser's desk

44 1. I don't know--I do know...(and give correct answer). 2. Opposite answer--No, and give correct answer 3. Refusal to speak--That's right...and give correct answer. 4. I don't care.--I care enough about you for both of us. 5. Personal insult or racial slur a). Temporarily ignore b). Give correct answer c). Deal with slur/insult at end

45

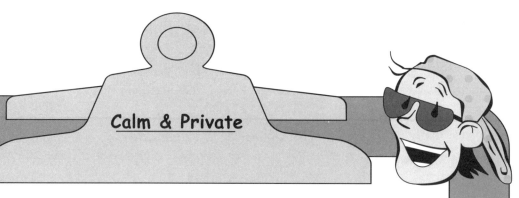

Calm & Private

1. "Thank you for leaving your (<u>math</u>) class. I'd like to talk with you for a moment. I think you know Mr./Ms.Jones who also teaches here. (Have a witness, if possible.)

2. Please take a seat. (<u>Name</u>),do you know the reason for this meeting? (wait) Do you think it's to help you to succeed or fail?

3. (If the student looks upset or is angrily looking away...) Do I look angry? (wait) **I am not angry.**

4. (<u>Name</u>), have we spoken a lot about how important it is that you pass my class? (wait) Let's talk about your learning. What grade would you like to make in my class?

5. Think about this: (pause) When you continue to (<u>name problem</u>), does it help you to reach your goal or does it hurt you?

6. If you could erase everything and begin again, what would you do differently?

7. When are you going to start doing it?

8. I know you can be successful. You are very capable, (<u>Name</u>).

9. We will meet immediately should there be another problem.

10. Thank you, (<u>Name</u>)." (Shake hands.)

Enhance the Vision© - Chapter 5 - EV05
Six Ways to Roll Up Your Sleeves the Right Way

©1994 Diana Day Training
www.dianaday.com • 972-287-7773

You Can Do--but it's up to YOU!

NAME _____ GRADE/CLASS _____ DATE _____

Parents' names _____ Daytime phone #'s_____

1

What grades do YOU want to make?

I want to _____

_____

_____

_____

Report Card A+

2

What are you doing that's holding you back?

I am _____

_____

_____

_____.

3

Knowing what you want and what's holding you back, your goal is to

_____

_____

_____

_____

GOAL

FINISH

4

What steps will you take to make this happen?

1. _____
2. _____
3. _____

GOAL

HIT THE BOOKS IN STYLE

5

When will you begin?

I will start _____.

URGENT

6

GO FOR IT!

If you get down on yourself, what will you say to encourage yourself?

_____

_____

_____

EXPECT SUCCESS

47

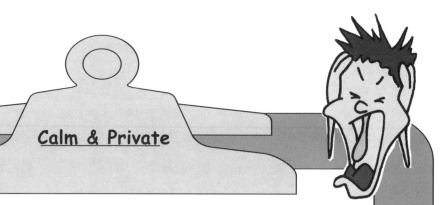

Calm & Private

1. "Thank you for leaving your (<u>Math</u>) class. I'd like for us to go back to my class to talk for a moment. I think you remember Mr./Ms.Jones. Please take a seat.

2. (<u>Name</u>), you (<u>stayed in your seat and worked</u>) for three days, but today you (<u>did little work and visited friends</u>).

3. We continue to meet because I believe in you. I know you can be successful. Let's talk about your (<u>grades/behavior</u>) and what's happening in my class. What do you think your grades/behavior should be?

4. What is your plan to meet these goals? What can I do to help you?
   (Be prepared with suggestions and role-play them.
   Show PACE form (page 36) if appropriate.)

5. (<u>Name</u>), as your teacher, I can't allow you to throw away your future, and affect other students' learning and their futures.

6. When you refuse directions and (<u>do not work and bother others</u>), then you will (<u>need to learn in another location than my room</u>).

7. What will happen if you refuse to follow directions?
   What will happen if you follow directions? (Get an education)

8. We will meet with the Assistant Principal should you refuse to cooperate.

9. (<u>Name</u>), I know you can be successful. I believe in you. Do you believe in you? Put your hand in mine. Let's shake."

48

Find the Finish Line--One Step at a Time

NAME _____ GRADE/CLASS _____ DATE _____

Parent's Names _____ Daytime phone # _____

STEP 1
Have I talked with you a lot or a little about
the challenge you're having in class? _____

STEP 2
Do you think I care about your success? _____
How do you know that? _____

STEP 3
Do you understand the reason I cannot allow
you to continue to do what you're doing? _____
What is the reason? _____
_____

STEP 4
Do you still want the goal we discussed? _____

STEP 5
Which action steps do you need to focus upon to make
sure you reach your goal? _____
_____
_____

STEP 6
What will happen if you do not help yourself?
_____
_____

STEP 7
What will you do differently to help yourself be successful?
_____
_____

_____
Signature

Enhance the Vision© - Chapter 5 - EV05
Six Ways to Roll Up Your Sleeves the Right Way

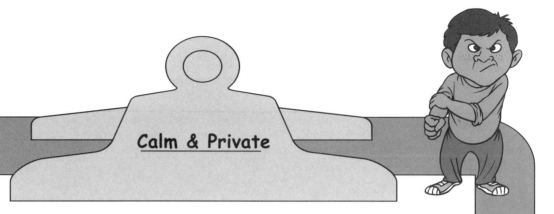

Calm & Private

1. "Thank you for leaving your (<u>math</u>) class. I'd like to talk with you for a few minutes. Do you remember Mr./Ms. Jones?

2. (<u>Name</u>), you (<u>did your work</u>) for four days, but today you (<u>refused to work</u>).

3. I still believe in you. I know you can be successful. We have discussed your (<u>learning/behavior</u>) goals. Do you still want to reach them?

4. We also discussed what would happen if you continued your misbehavior of (<u>refusal to work</u>). It is stopping you and others from being successful.

5. It's time for a written contract where you and I will decide what will happen if you continue to (<u>name the problem</u>). We will write it together because it's y-o-u-r plan.

6. Do you realize that you have the power to reach your goals and have a future?

7. I am here ... to help you. Can I do it for you? I cannot do it for you. Only you can change and become the person you really want to be. Let's shake."

Enhance the Vision© - Chapter 5 - EV05
Six Ways to Roll Up Your Sleeves the Right Way

©1994 Diana Day Training
www.dianaday.com • 972-287-7773

Responsibility Agreement

NAME _____ GRADE/CLASS _____ DATE _____

Parents' names _____ Daytime phone #'s _____

Are you getting tired of these talks? _____

Do you think we care about you? _____

How do you know that? _____

Do you care about you? _____

Why do you say that? _____
_____

FUTURE AHEAD

What more can we do to help you? _____
_____
_____

WRITE IT DOWN

It's Time for a Contract

I _____ need to _____.
your name

To accomplish this, I plan to:

1._____

2._____

3._____

4._____

If I am unsuccessful, I believe this should happen:

1._____

2._____

3._____

"If it's to be, it's up to ME."

I will need this help from others:

1._____

2._____

3._____

Signature

Enhance the Vision© - Chapter 5 - EV05
Six Ways to Roll Up Your Sleeves the Right Way

©1994 Diana Day Training
www.dianaday.com • 972-287-7773

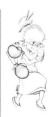

Refuser Script #4

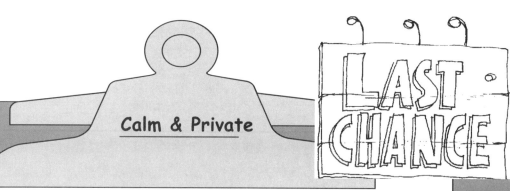

Calm & Private

At the Meeting
Parent(s), Administrator, Counselor, Teacher(s)

Before the Meeting

- Plan the role each person will have at the meeting.
  Decide what is the desired outcome for this meeting.

- Have name cards and verbal introductions for each person.
  When family member(s) arrive, student sits in the outer
  office and is not a part of the meeting *at this time.*

The Meeting with Parents

1. (Start on a positive note.)
   "We want you to know that we care about (<u>Student</u>).
   We also know that you care about him/her, too.
   We appreciate that you (<u>got off work early today,
   borrowed a car, have sick children at home</u>) and are here."

2. "The reason we are concerned is (<u>show and explain
   documentation</u>). We know that you will be concerned, too."

3. Briefly explain what has been done to help student.

4. Show the student's worksheets from pages 47, 49 and 51.
   and the "Contract." Thoroughly explain the impact of continued
   misbehavior and in what ways teachers are supporting the student.

Enhance the Vision© - Chapter 5 - EV05
Six Ways to Roll Up Your Sleeves the Right Way

©1994 Diana Day Training
www.dianaday.com • 972-287-7773

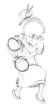

Calm & Private

5. Get agreement of parents to have supervised study/restriction time for their child in keeping with the "Responsibility Contract" (page 54). Explain the importance of encouragement for their child to reach his/her goals. Explain exactly what will happen if the student continues (possible retention, out-of-school suspension, alternative school or boot camp).

The Meeting with Parents and Student

6. Student is brought into meeting. Parents discuss their plan-of-action and ask for input from their child to help him/her succeed. They explain what will happen if (<u>name the problem</u>) doesn't stop.

7. Check for understanding of student to be sure he/she understands the plan.

8. All attendees sign the agreement. If the student refuses to sign the agreement, it is still in effect.

9. A follow-up meeting date is set to give parents feedback. Parents are to tell you how and where they are to be contacted if the student does not follow the agreement terms. This is said in front of the student.

10. "(<u>Name</u>), know that all of us are working to help you and care about your success. We expect your cooperation. Your future depends on your willingness to succeed."

11. Handshakes. Someone walks parent(s) to front door of school.

Enhance the Vision© - Chapter 5 - EV05
Six Ways to Roll Up Your Sleeves the Right Way

©1994 Diana Day Training
www.dianaday.com • 972-287-7773

Contract of Mutual Responsibility

Student _____ Subject/Grade_____

Chronic off-task behavior: _____

_____

_____

In order to continue to learn with your class, it will be necessary for

_____ to demonstrate consistently the following responsibilities:

**S
T
U
D
E
N
T**

1. _____

2. _____

3. _____

4. _____

5. _____

_____
Signature/Date

**P
A
R
E
N
T
(s)**

The parents' responsibility is:

1. _____

2. _____

3. _____

_____   _____
Signature/Date   Signature/Date

**T
E
A
C
H
E
R**

The teacher's responsibility is:

1. _____

2. _____

3. _____

_____
Signature/Date

54

Conflict Resolution Form

Name _____ Date _____

W H A T ?

What happened to start the conflict? _____

_____

_____

W H Y ?

Why do you think the other person(s) argued or fought with you?

_____

_____

_____

Why did you argue or fight with the other person? _____

_____

_____

_____

P L A N ?

Did arguing or fighting solve the problem? _____
List three things you can do differently if this happens again.

    1. _____

    2. _____

    3. _____

W H E N

What can you do and say to the person(s) you argued or fought
with to make things better?_____

_____

_____

When will you start to make things better? _____

Enhance the Vision© - Chapter 5 - EV05
Six Ways to Roll Up Your Sleeves the Right Way

©1994 Diana Day Training
www.dianaday.com • 972-287-7773

C. BARKER © 1994

DIANA DAY WORK HOP

'I said look like an EAGLE.......not a BEAGLE!'

Diana Day taught in the following places:

Watts - Los Angeles, CA · Highland Park - East Los Angeles, CA
Hawaiian Gardens - Downtown Los Angeles · Chinatown - Downtown Los Angeles
Federal Projects - Detroit, MI · Dearborn, MI · Melvindale, MI

These are some humorous quotes from her students (K-12).

Who was Johnny Appleseed? "A man who scattered his seed all over the country."

Who is the First Lady? "Eve."

"Slush is snow with all the fun melted out."

"The Earth holds onto everything with its grabity."

"The Pony Express was a system worked out to send ponies through the mail."

"Marconi invented the noodle and stuff like that."

"* is an asterisk. It is a reminder to go look someplace else if you want to know the whole truth."

"Polite means to say thank you when you really mean it."

"Now that the dinosaurs are safely dead, we can call them clumsee and stoopid."

"A parakeet is a friendly bird. He will eat seeds or your hand."

"By the time we finally arrived at my uncle's house I was ready
to eat anything. Needless to say, I was eager to see my new baby cousin."

Chapter 6

Four Methods to Ensure Easy & Effective Documentation

- Documentation that Will Protect You

- How to Avoid Parent Showdowns with Compelling Records

- Chronicle Misbehavior with Specificity in Just Seconds

If you want cooperation, support colleagues' ideas as enthusiastically as you do your own.

–Diana Day
Texas Elementary Principals' and Supervisors' Association Meeting, June 1994

"To get a full share of commitment from others, multiply their involvement and divide the pleasure."

–Diana Day
West Valley Superintendents Meeting, Pendergast, Arizona, November 2003

If you expect to climb the ladder of success, secure it to a strong foundation

–Diana Day
National Middle School Conference, Washington D.C. - November 2002

You have choices in the education profession, take it or leave it.

–Diana Day
Texas Elementary Principals' and Supervisors' Association Meeting, June 1996

Happiness is not a guarantee.
All you get is time and space.
It's up to you to fill it with joy.

–Diana Day
"The Visions Binder© --Goal Setting: From Dreams to Reality"

You want job security?
Always be worth more than you're paid.

–Diana Day
Attorney General's Conference, Honolulu, Hawaii - April 1996

"There is serious violence in U.S. schools. When teachers truly consider what is in the best interest of their students, and convey this message to them through meaningful intervention, we will embrace one another with respect and trust. They are our future and we are theirs."

–Diana Day
National Association of Elementary School Principals - April 2003

Enhance the Vision© - Chapter 6 - EV06
Four Methods to Ensure Easy & Effective Documentation

©1994 Diana Day Training
www.dianaday.com · 972-287-7773

Are You Too Busy to Be Effective?

Are there so many demands upon your time that one extra duty could sink your ship? Sometimes you have demands put upon you that are small, but they require supreme organization to keep your nose above the waterline. If you are not organized, the small things can overwhelm you.

Have you ever eaten a side of beef? Probably not. Have you ever eaten a handful of chips? Two handfuls? Three? Probably so. It's the small things that can get to you. Don't be overwhelmed by the small things that can consume your life.

90-10 RULE

Peter Drucker, a famous economist, pointed out that 90% of our time is spent with matters of low importance. Only 10% of our time is spent focused on high priorities. It appears we are doing things backwards!

A Prescription For "Schedulosis"

Careful documentation of student behavior is vital.

Some teachers spend hours recopying data. Accurate documentation is essential if a parent questions an academic or conduct grade. On the following pages are samples of forms that will make recording easy and will yield a high return in administrator, parent and student support.

Pg 60 - 6 or 9 Week Record Sheet

Pg 62 - Weekly Behavior Summary

Pg 64 - Quarterly Conduct Chart

Pg 66 - Documentation in a Notebook

Enhance the Vision© - Chapter 6 - EV06
Four Methods to Ensure Easy & Effective Documentation

©1994 Diana Day Training
www.dianaday.com • 972-287-7773

6 or 9 Week Record Sheet

Rest Room   Nurse

M	T	W	T	F	M	T	W	T	F	M	T	W	T	F

M	T	W	T	F	M	T	W	T	F	M	T	W	T	F

M	T	W	T	F	M	T	W	T	F	M	T	W	T	F

60

Enhance the Vision© - Chapter 6 - EV06
Four Methods to Ensure Easy & Effective Documentation

©1994 Diana Day Training
www.dianaday.com • 972-287-7773

6 or 9 Week Record Sheet

Rest Room   Nurse

IMA N. TRUBEL					URA OUTTAGETME					I. DIDNTDOIT				
M	T	W	T	F	M	T	W	T	F	M	T	W	T	F
	24		6/1							2				
1	6/1		3							2				
1			6/1		/	/	/	/	/					
1		/		6/1										
						◣				2				
1	6/1		6/1	/										
							/							
			/									/		

REGULAR EXPECTATIONS

1. Be in your assigned seat/area, ready to work when the bell finishes ringing.
2. Have paper, pencil, books and all needed materials every day.
3. HFBO--Keep hands, feet, books &. objects to yourself.
4. No profanity, rude gestures, cruel teasing or put downs.
5. Follow the directions of any adult working at this school.

6. CRITICAL EXPECTATIONS

1. Fighting or threatening to fight
2. Damaging or destroying student, teacher or school property
3. Overtly refusing to do school work when capable by throwing materials, tipping over furniture or yelling
4. Engaging in behavior that creates an unsafe situation, is sexually provocative or shuts down your ability to teach or students ability to learn

6/1 = Critical/Fighting

M	T	W	T	F	M	T	W	T	F	M	T	W	T	F

61

Enhance the Vision© - Chapter 6 - EV06
Four Methods to Ensure Easy & Effective Documentation

©1994 Diana Day Training
www.dianaday.com • 972-287-7773

Weekly Behavior Summary

Teacher _____ Grade _____ Date _____

STUDENT	EXPECTATION BROKEN	LEARNING CHOICES	COMMENTS
1. _____	_ _ _ _ _ _ _ _ _	RA RA RA BR BR TC PC O	_____
2. _____	_ _ _ _ _ _ _ _ _	RA RA RA BR BR TC PC O	_____
3. _____	_ _ _ _ _ _ _ _ _	RA RA RA BR BR TC PC O	_____
4. _____	_ _ _ _ _ _ _ _ _	RA RA RA BR BR TC PC O	_____
5. _____	_ _ _ _ _ _ _ _ _	RA RA RA BR BR TC PC O	_____
6. _____	_ _ _ _ _ _ _ _ _	RA RA RA BR BR TC PC O	_____
7. _____	_ _ _ _ _ _ _ _ _	RA RA RA BR BR TC PC O	_____
8. _____	_ _ _ _ _ _ _ _ _	RA RA RA BR BR TC PC O	_____
9. _____	_ _ _ _ _ _ _ _ _	RA RA RA BR BR TC PC O	_____
10. _____	_ _ _ _ _ _ _ _ _	RA RA RA BR BR TC PC O	_____
11. _____	_ _ _ _ _ _ _ _ _	RA RA RA BR BR TC PC O	_____
12. _____	_ _ _ _ _ _ _ _ _	RA RA RA BR BR TC PC O	_____
13. _____	_ _ _ _ _ _ _ _ _	RA RA RA BR BR TC PC O	_____
14. _____	_ _ _ _ _ _ _ _ _	RA RA RA BR BR TC PC O	_____
15. _____	_ _ _ _ _ _ _ _ _	RA RA RA BR BR TC PC O	_____
16. _____	_ _ _ _ _ _ _ _ _	RA RA RA BR BR TC PC O	_____
17. _____	_ _ _ _ _ _ _ _ _	RA RA RA BR BR TC PC O	_____
18. _____	_ _ _ _ _ _ _ _ _	RA RA RA BR BR TC PC O	_____
19. _____	_ _ _ _ _ _ _ _ _	RA RA RA BR BR TC PC O	_____
20. _____	_ _ _ _ _ _ _ _ _	RA RA RA BR BR TC PC O	_____
21. _____	_ _ _ _ _ _ _ _ _	RA RA RA BR BR TC PC O	_____
22. _____	_ _ _ _ _ _ _ _ _	RA RA RA BR BR TC PC O	_____
23. _____	_ _ _ _ _ _ _ _ _	RA RA RA BR BR TC PC O	_____
24. _____	_ _ _ _ _ _ _ _ _	RA RA RA BR BR TC PC O	_____
25. _____	_ _ _ _ _ _ _ _ _	RA RA RA BR BR TC PC O	_____

RA=Refocus Area   **BR**=Buddy Room*   **TC**=Team Conference
PC=Parent Conference/Contact **O**=Office   **LR**=Loss of Recess
D=Detention   **HA**=Hands To Self   **TB**=Talking Back   **NB**=No Book
NP=No Paper   **FE**=Feet to Self   **OS**=Out of Seat   **PD**=Put Down
SP=Spitting   **H**=Hitting   **RFD**=Refusal to Follow Directions

*Buddy Room--
See VISION
MANAGEMENT©
Pages 110-112

Enhance the Vision© - Chapter 6 - EV06
Four Methods to Ensure Easy & Effective Documentation

©1994 Diana Day Training
www.dianaday.com • 972-287-7773

Weekly Behavior Summary

Teacher _____ Grade _____ Date _____

	STUDENT	EXPECTATION BROKEN	LEARNING CHOICES	COMMENTS
1.	Acheman, Troy	_ _ _ _ _ _ _	RA RA RA BR BR TC PC O	Perfect!
2.	Alec, Smarty	5 _ _ _ _ _ _	(RA) RA RA BR BR TC PC O	TB=Talking Back
3.	Brane, Burd		RA RA RA BR BR TC PC O	
4.	Clinton, Willy	3 3 3 _ _ _ _	(RA)(RA)(RA) BR BR TC PC O	HA=Hands to Self
5.	Dillon, Matt		RA RA RA BR BR TC PC O	
6.	Dooit, Diddint	3 5 4 _ _ _ _	(RA)(RA)(RA) BR BR TC PC O	H=Hitting, TB, PD
7.	Donner, Blitzen	1 _ _ _ _ _ _	(RA) RA RA BR BR TC PC O	Tardy-Hid in bathroom
8.	Gerbels, Dozzinoff	Critical _ _ _ _	RA RA RA BR BR TC PC(O)	Smoking
9.	Heddell, Gordie	2 3 3 _ _ _ _	(RA)(RA)(RA) BR BR TC PC O	NP, SP, HA
10.	Lawrence, Keith		RA RA RA BR BR TC PC O	Perfect!
11.	Murphy, Ed. E.	4 4 4 4 _ _ _	(RA)(RA)(RA)(BR)(BR) TC PC O	FE, OS, TB, TB, TB
12.	Nuthin, Idontwannado		RA RA RA BR BR TC PC O	
13.	Pumphandle, Ann Teek		RA RA RA BR BR TC PC O	
14.	Sampson, Delilah	5 5 5 5 5 _ _	(RA)(RA)(RA)(BR)(BR) TC PC O	Lied RFD
15.	Soprano, Alto		RA RA RA BR BR TC PC O	
16.	Soprano, Tony	Critical _ _ _ _	RA RA RA BR BR TC PC(O)	Fighting
17.	Vittles, Crummie	5 _ _ _ _ _ _	(RA) RA RA BR BR TC PC O	TB
18.	Young, Wannabe	5 _ _ _ _ _ _	(RA) RA RA BR BR TC PC O	Playing w/TV
19.	Zitts, Manny		RA RA RA BR BR TC PC O	
20.	Zitts, Manny Moore		RA RA RA BR BR TC PC O	
21.			RA RA RA BR BR TC PC O	
22.			RA RA RA BR BR TC PC O	
23.			RA RA RA BR BR TC PC O	
24.			RA RA RA BR BR TC PC O	
25.			RA RA RA BR BR TC PC O	

RA=Refocus Area   **BR**=Buddy Room*   **TC**=Team Conference
PC=Parent Conference/Contact **O**=Office   **LR**=Loss of Recess
D=Detention   **HA**=Hands To Self   **TB**=Talking Back   **NB**=No Book
NP=No Paper   **FE**=Feet to Self   **OS**=Out of Seat   **PD**=Put Down
SP=Spitting   **H**=Hitting   **RFD**=Refusal to Follow Directions

*Buddy Room--
See VISION
MANAGEMENT©
Pages 110-112

Enhance the Vision© - Chapter 6 - EV06
Four Methods to Ensure Easy & Effective Documentation

©1994 Diana Day Training
www.dianaday.com • 972-287-7773

Quarterly Conduct Chart

Name	
100% EXCELLENT	
99	
98	
97	
96	
95	
94	
93	
92	
91	
90	
SATISFACTORY	
89	
88	
87	
86	
85	
84	
83	
82	
81	
80	
NEEDS IMPROVEMENT	
79	
78	
77	
76	
75	
74	
73	
72	
71	
70	
UNSATISFACTORY	
69	
68	

Name	
100% EXCELLENT	
99	
98	
97	
96	
95	
94	
93	
92	
91	
90	
SATISFACTORY	
89	
88	
87	
86	
85	
84	
83	
82	
81	
80	
NEEDS IMPROVEMENT	
79	
78	
77	
76	
75	
74	
73	
72	
71	
70	
UNSATISFACTORY	
69	
68	

Enhance the Vision© - Chapter 6 - EV06
Four Methods to Ensure Easy & Effective Documentation

©1994 Diana Day Training
www.dianaday.com • 972-287-7773

Quarterly Conduct Chart

NAME	INTA EVERYTHANG		
100%	EXCELLENT		
99	3/2	5	Spilled class ant farm
98	3/2	5	Tore up two worksheets
97	3/3	3	Hit two students
96	3/4	3	Ran from sub
95	3/4	4	Called aide "butthead"
94	3/4	3	Put rabbits, Ozzie & Harriet, in same cage
93			
92			
91			
90			
	SATISFACTORY		
89			
88	Three documentations in any day = **a parent contact.**		
87			
86			
85			
84			
83			
82			
81			
80			
	NEEDS IMPROVEMENT		
79			
78			
77			
76			
75			
74			
73			
72			
71			
70			
	UNSATISFACTORY		
69			
68			

NAME	GOTYA COVERED		
100%	EXCELLENT		
99	4/1	1	Tardy - Playing in bathroom
98			
97			
96			
95			
94			
93			
92			
91			
90			
	SATISFACTORY		
89			
88			
87			
86			
85			
84			
83			
82			
81			
80			
	NEEDS IMPROVEMENT		
79			
78			
77			
76			
75			
74			
73			
72			
71			
70			
	UNSATISFACTORY		
69			
68			

Enhance the Vision© - Chapter 6 - EV06
Four Methods to Ensure Easy & Effective Documentation

©1994 Diana Day Training
www.dianaday.com • 972-287-7773

Documentation in a Notebook

Name of Student	Date Class	Expectation not followed	Learning Choice

Enhance the Vision© - Chapter 6 - EV06
Four Methods to Ensure Easy & Effective Documentation

©1994 Diana Day Training
www.dianaday.com • 972-287-7773

Documentation in a Notebook

Name of Student	Date/ Class	Which Expectation not followed?	What Happens Next?
Betty Weber	Sept. 19/ English	Was late Expectation #1	30 seconds after class to discuss how to be on time
Betty Weber	Nov. 3/ English	No book Expectation #3	Shared a book Worked for Librarian 30 minutes
Betty Weber	May 23/ English	Not being silent during test Expectation #5	Talked to teacher in private Note to parents to be signed

Enhance the Vision© - Chapter 6 - EV06
Four Methods to Ensure Easy & Effective Documentation

©1994 Diana Day Training
www.dianaday.com • 972-287-7773

- **MAPS** (Use MAPS before each transition and new lesson format.)
- **DBA** (Desired Behavior Acknowledgement--Teacher acknowledges the students who perform the task correctly.)
- **"Moe" Praise** (praise a student to the right and the left of the student who is not on-task. When the non-performer does the task, praise him/her.)
- **Walk a Path** (Circulate around the room to make sure that students are doing what you requested.)
- **Delayed Approval** (Keep an index card in your pocket and wear a neck pen to make notes about students who are following directions. Read after the lesson is finished for elementary or privately for secondary.)

For students who continue to refuse after having been redirected:
- Build a Bridge (direct the class to an independent activity)
- Divide and Conquer (reinforce students around the refuser)
- Be an Eagle--Bend over at the refuser's desk, and say,
- "(Name), the direction was to ..."
- "I want," "I need," "I expect" you to _____."
- Walk Away (Do not stay and wait to have a confrontation.)

- To stop arguers, say, *"I understand that…"* or *"I know that…"*
- Big Eyes to stop misbehavior (open your eyes widely and do not smile.)
- Expectant Eyes to start desired behavior (open your eyes widely, smile, nod.)
- Nod as you are giving a student one-on-one directions.

- Stand to discipline; sit to counsel
- Lean over to be at the student's eye level
- Remember, use three voice levels
    (loud--whole class, medium--small group,
    soft--one-on-one)
- Two-finger touch to gain student's attention

ALLRIGHT!

Remember the "Four B's" and you can be the master of your classroom!
1. "B" KIND   2. "B" FIRM
3. "B" FAIR   4. "B" CONSISTENT

If I Could Live It Over...

Written by Nadine Stair when she was age 87.

If I had my life to live over again,

I'd dare to make more mistakes next time.

I'd relax.

I would limber up.

I would be sillier than I have been on this trip.

I would take fewer things seriously.

I would take more chances.

I would take more trips. I would climb more mountains, swim more rivers.

I would eat more ice cream and a lot less beans.

I would, perhaps, have more actual troubles, but I'd have fewer imaginary ones.

You see, I'm one of those people who lives seriously and sanely, hour after hour,

     day after day.

Oh, I've had my moments. And, if I had it to do all over again, I'd have more of them.

In fact, I'd try to have nothing else, just moments, one after another, instead of

     living so many years ahead of each day.

I've been one of those persons who never goes anywhere without a thermometer, a hot

     water bottle, a raincoat, and a parachute.

If I had to do it again, I would travel lighter than I have.

If I had my life to live over, I would start barefoot earlier in the spring

     and stay that way in the fall.

I would go to more dances.

I would ride more merry-go-rounds.

I would pick more daisies.

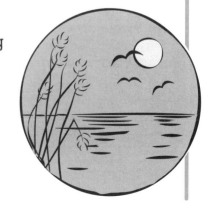

Enhance the Vision© - Chapter 6 - EV06
Four Methods to Ensure Easy & Effective Documentation

©1994 Diana Day Training
www.dianaday.com • 972-287-7773

> *Give students **discipline** and you've made **your day** better.*
>
> *Teach students **self-discipline** and you've made **their lives** better.*

VISION MANAGEMENT©
TEACHING BRAIN-COMPATIBLE SELF-MANAGEMENT

More than merely a philosophy, Diana Day's *Vision Management©*, is a comprehensive, research-based series of programs consisting of specific brain-compatible strategies that integrate into teaching:

- **Brain-Based Behavior Management**
- **Student Responsibility**
- **Conflict Resolution**
- **Social Skills**
- **Problem-Solving**
- **Character Development**
- **Whole School Reform**
- **Self-Management**

Vision Management© is a discipline plan that creates schoolwide consistency and guides students to become self-managers. *Vision Management©* improves schools by:

➤ **Increasing test scores**
➤ **Reducing office referrals by 49-87%**
➤ **Taking schools from low-performing to exemplary in two years!**

Vision Management© meshes seamlessly with existing management programs that need more substance & structure while stimulating whole school reform efforts. Teachers, new and veteran, rave about the immediate improvement after learning the hands-on, classroom-proven strategies gleaned from *Vision Management©* training.

TRAINING

FOR EDUCATORS

VISION MANAGEMENT© (Blue Book)
Create a Consistent Campuswide Discipline Plan Using Brain-Compatible Methods that Teach K-8 Self-Management

ENHANCE THE VISION©-*Hands-On Tools & Techniques* (Red Book)
100's of Strategies for Students Who Refuse & Disrespect

MANAGING CHALLENGING STUDENTS© (Teal Book)
How to Succeed with the Most Difficult Students

EFFECTIVE PARENT CONFERENCES© (Purple Book)
Turn Tough Parents into Cooperative Partners

BRAIN VISION© (Green Book)
Brain-Compatible Strategies that Engage 100% of Kids

TEAM VISION©
Increase Collaboration, Loyalty & Communication of Staff

FUTURE VISION©
A Secondary Discipline Management System for 9th-12th

FOR ADMINISTRATORS & BOARD

3 PROGRAMS FOR ADMINISTRATORS:
"How to Handle Discipline as an Administrative Team"
"The 10 Most Common Mistakes That Leaders Make"
"Team Vision - Improve Communication & Collaboration"

VISIONARY SCHOOL BOARDS© TRAINING
Get the Board "On Board" with Better Communication & Support

FOR PARENTS & PARAPROFESSIONALS

911 FOR PARENTS©
Train Parents to Manage Kids & Support Your Efforts

NO HASSLE HOMEWORK©
Teach Parents How to End the Homework Struggle

911 FOR BUS DRIVERS© - BEHAVIOR MANAGEMENT
Bring Safety & Sanity to Your Transportation Program

911 FOR LUNCH MONITORS© - BEHAVIOR MANAGEMENT
Cafeteria Personnel Learn to Manage Kids Effectively

PLUS
911 FOR PARENTS VIDEO KIT TRAINING (FOR COUNSELORS, PARENT LIAISONS AND ADMINISTRATORS)
MENTOR TRAINING, MEMORABLE KEYNOTES, COLLEGE COURSES, STAFF RETREATS AND CONSULTING

E-mail: goals@dianaday.com • Web site: www.dianaday.com
2903 Saturn Road • Garland, Texas 75041 • (972) 278-7773 • Fax (972) 278-8584

Mission Statement:

Our mission is to deliver exemplary discipline management training
and unique support materials to sustain positive behavior
by students at school and at home.

*"Give students discipline and you've made **your day** better.
Teach students self-discipline and you've made **their lives** better."*

Vision Management©

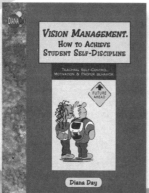

Educators K-12, Counselors, Spec. Education, New Teachers

- 96-Page Text Detailing How To Set-Up a Discipline Management Plan
- Supplies Discipline Link Missing From Character-Building Programs
- Features Student Self-Management, Self-Assessment With Many Reproducible Pages
- Used Campuswide, Has Decreased Office Referrals 49-89%

$19.95

Challenging Students©

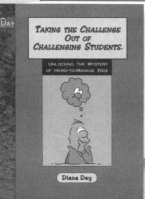

Educators K-12, Counselors, Spec. Education, New Teachers

- 80-Page Text Unlocks The Mystery of the "Hard-to-Manage"
- Be a Successful Teacher With Unmotivated, Demanding and Difficult Students
- Steps to Avoid Being Hooked Into a Confrontation
- How To Reverse Repeated Misbehavior
- Master The "7 Steps to Teach a New Behavior"

$19.95

Pencil Holder

Imprinted with "Is your Vision focused on your goals?"
A great start-the-year or appreciation gift for staff!
Holds any pen or pencil. White/royal blue.
Documentation at your fingertips!

$2.00

Intro to Vision Management© Audio Tape

$9.95

Helpful discipline management reminders for
new teachers to listen to on the way to school.
Great daily reminders for daily success!

Posters

Dedication Poster - (blue):
For Teacher Commitment to Help
Students Succeed

Management Plan - (yellow):
Preprinted Behavior
Management Plan

$2.25 ea.

shop online www.dianaday.com

Desktop Mentor©

Educators K-12, Spec. Education, New Teachers

72 Answers to The Most-Asked Questions in Behavior Management in an Easy-Reference Spiral Book.

· How To Set-Up an Effective Discipline Management System

· Handling Back-Talk, Disputes, Incomplete Work

· Stopping Disrespect, Tattling, Bullying

· Responses for Refusal, Arguments between Students

An indispensable tool for new and veteran teachers alike!

Say, "I am going to teach you an experiment about vibration. Everyone take your hand and place four fingers…not just your fingertips, your fingers… on your throat. When I give the signal, say your name aloud 2 times. Feel the vibration your vocal cords make on your fingers! How many of you felt the vibration? Vibration means you were NOT whispering."

"This time , when I give the signal, say your name so only your work partner can hear it…a whisper. You will NOT feel any vibrations on your fingers if your are whispering. CONGRATULATIONS, you have just learned how to whisper!"

13. WHISPER VOICE: HOW TO TEACH IT

$19.95

Day 2 Day© Motivational Messages

Best Seller!

Principals, Educators K-8, Counselors, Spec. Education, New Teachers

One-Minute Intercom Messages that Inspire

· 180 Interactive, Often Humorous, Always Thought-Provoking Announcements

· Weekly Themes With Word-of-The-Week

· Focus Students and Teachers on Self-Improvement

· Build Character, Values, Manners, Respect and Teamwork by Using as 2-5 Minute Lessons

$29.95 $29.95

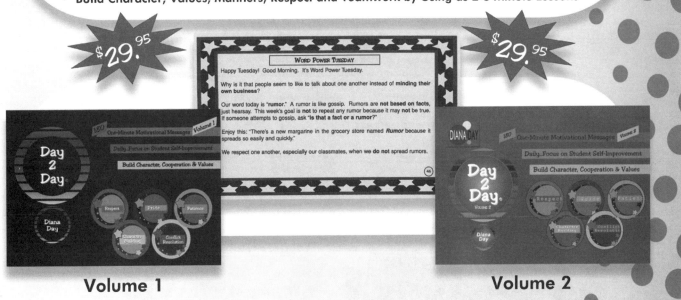

Volume 1   Volume 2

Goal For It!© K-4

Educators K-4, Counselors, Spec. Education

- 39 Powerful Lessons That Establish a Complete Discipline System
- Stories and Lessons Teach Why There Are Rules and Consequences
- Plus, Celebrating Success, Goal-Setting, Never Giving Up, Handling Bullies, Resolving Conflict, How To Think Before You Act
- Book Comes With 2 Plush Puppets

$19.95

Goal For It!© 5-12

Educators 5-12, Counselors, Spec. Education

Perfect book for ADVISORY or Health classes where teachers value quick, meaningful hero stories that motivate and inspire, complete with questions/answers and short activity.

Teaches necessity of rules, boundaries, having good character, self-motivation, goal-setting, never giving up, overcoming hardship, recognizing opportunity and believing in oneself.

$16.95

Visions Character-Building Binder©

Educators K-8, Counselors

**A Year of Weekly Lessons for K-3 and 4-8 That Teach:
Putting Out Effort, Respectfulness, Recognizing Opportunities,
Patience, Celebrating Success, Being Responsible**

- 72 Lessons (36 for K-3 and 36 for 4-8) for How To Goal-Set & Improve Character & Respectfulness
- Interactive, Fun Lessons With Overlay Masters & Worksheets
    - Buy One Binder and Get School Site License to Reproduce for Each Classroom
    - 4 Imprinted, Sectional Dividers for Your Reproduced Binders are Sold Separately

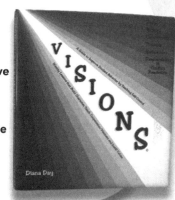

$249.95

shop online www.dianaday.com

911 For Parents© Live Performance

Sanity-Saving Skills to Take The Stress Out of Discipline at Home

Give parents a lifelong gift of training, taking frustration and stress out of discipline, creating calm, positive and meaningful interactions at home.

School groups, churches, hospitals and industry have sponsored the "911 for Parents" program for over 250,000 parents. Can be scheduled in any 2-3 hour time block.

We create your advertising masters and provide you, free-of-charge, "Getting Parents To Attend the '911 for Parents' Program." Call for information about this vital program.

2-3 hr. Live Performance

Diana with a parent, role-playing his son!

911 For Parents© Video Training Kit

Teachers & counselors use this video presentation, filmed with a live audience, to teach parents how to better manage their children. Create consistent discipline between home & school. Get parent support using four 30-minute, fast-paced videos.

Includes 4 Videos, 62-Page Leader's Guide and Parent Hand-Outs & Overlays in English & Spanish.

Best Seller!

$329.95

911 For Parents© Video-Viewing Set

The perfect tool to lend to all parents struggling with misbehaving children. Includes four 30-minute videos filled with humorous examples & valuable information in a sturdy storage case.

$99.95

Vision Management© Workshop

Educators K-12, Counselors, Spec. Education, Aides, Clerks

How To Achieve Student Self-Management

- Creates Competence, Cooperation & Consistency With All Staff Campuswide
- Increases On-Task Behavior and Improves Test Scores
- Supplies Discipline Link Missing From Character-Building Programs
- Teaches Student Self-Management and Self-Assessment
- Used Campuswide, Has Decreased Office Referrals 49-89%
- Includes a 96-Page Text Detailing How To Set-Up a Discipline Management Plan, a Management Plan Poster and a Teacher Dedication Poster

7 hr. Live Performance

Enhance The Vision© Workshop

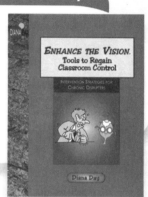

Educators K-12, Counselors, Spec. Education, Aides, Clerks

Tools To Regain Classroom Control

- Establish Effective Classroom Procedures That Prevent Problems Before They Begin
- Successful Strategies With Practice to Use With Students Who Refuse, Disrupt and Disrespect
- End Student Back-Talk, Disputes Between Students and Arguments With Teachers

7 hr. Live Performance

Challenging Students© Workshop

Educators K-12, Counselors, Spec. Education, Aides, Clerks

Unlocking The Mystery of Hard-to-Manage Kids

- How to Refocus & Manage Difficult, Distracted and Troubled Students
- Be a Successful Teacher With Unmotivated, Demanding and Difficult Students
- Steps to Avoid Being Hooked Into a Confrontation
- How to Reverse Repeated Misbehavior
- Master the "7 Steps to Teach a New Behavior"
- Includes 80-Page Text That Will Help Students Succeed

7 hr. Live Performance

Effective Parent Conferences© Workshop

Educators K-12, Counselors, Spec. Education, Aides, Clerks

Improve Student Behavior Through Conferencing, Calling and Communicating

- Unique Strategies to Conference, Call and Communicate With Uncooperative Parents
- Powerful Words That Prompt Cooperation
- Useful Scripts to Use for Challenging Situations

7 hr. Live Performance

shop online www.dianaday.com

discipline management made easy

911 For Bus Drivers© Workshop

Behavior Management Training for Transportation Specialists

A Fun and Informative 2-1/2 - 3 Hour Program That Will:

- **Create a Positive Climate, Competence and Consistency in Behavior Management with Drivers**
- **Lower Turnover Rate of Drivers**
- **Reduce Vandalism to Buses**
- **Avoid Escalating Confrontations**

3-4 hr. Live Performance

911© For Lunch Monitors Workshop

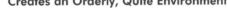

Success Strategies for Managing Your Cafeteria

A Detailed, Informative 3-hour Session That:

- **Organizes Your Cafeteria for Success**
- **Instills Confidence, Competence and Consistency**
- **Creates an Orderly, Quite Environment**

3 hr. Live Performance

Administrative Leadership Series©

Train your anagement team or School Board with 3 - 6 hour training at your site or on retreat.

- **"How To Handle Discipline As An Administrative Team©"**
- **"The 10 Most Common Mistakes That Leaders Make©"**
- **"Team Vision©: How to Get Cooperation, Better Communication and Collaboration From Uncooperative People"**

3-6 hr. Live Performance

Workshop Details

<u>Length</u>: 1/2 to full-day programs

<u>Materials</u>: Complete with bound, interactive workbooks or packets

<u>Cost</u>: Call today for a quote!

Get a FREE Day2Day© Volume 1 when you schedule your workshop & say "discipline management made easy"!

For More Information

about any of these dynamic workshops, or to order materials, contact us TODAY!

Diana Day Training Center
P.O. Box 472283
Garland, Texas 75047-2283
972.278.7773 · fax 972.278.8584
goals@dianaday.com · www.dianaday.com

1. b) 2

2. Facial expression
   Tone of voice
   Volume
   Proximity
   Touch
   What you say (your attitude towards them)

3. c) To know what you expect student(s) to do at all times

4. b) False

5. Three a) loud   b) medium   c) soft

6. d) What's on the desk that should not be there

7. Four

8. "Eyes on me" or "Look at me."

9. Under your expectations, "Follow directions."

10. By having them put a "free-time activity" under their chair to work on when the assignment is finished.

11. "I understand that..." or "I know that..."

12. a) Redirect from across the room and continue to teach

13. Say, "I care enough about you for both of us" and then give the correct answer to your question. Or, "Can I make you care? You're right, I can't make you care."

14. b) Walk away

15. c) Writing them down

16. c) Do what is needed to stop the misbehavior, and discuss the problem with the student later

17. Say, "That's right" (as if student had given the correct answer) and then you give the correct answer.

18. Say, "I understand you want to talk about Shawn but we're not talking about Shawn. We're talking about you."

19. Three

20. c) Say, "I understand that you think it's not fair..."

21. a) After you have redirected and misbehavior continues

22. Two to three times depending on your grade level

23. To get parent support

24. b) four

25. At beginning of school year

C E L E B R A T I O N S	Answers for page 27	
	1. Clam Clap	6. WOW
	2. Wave	7. Big Daddy Pump
	3. Elvis	8. Sprinkler
	4. Navy Seals	9. Seal of Approval
	5. Texas Yee-Haw	10. The Standing "O"

DIANA DAY TRAINING PRODUCTS
discipline management made easy

2903 Saturn Road • Dept. EV04 • Garland, TX 75041
972-278-7773 • fax 972-278-8584
goals@dianaday.com • www.dianaday.com

PAGE #	ITEM		ITEM #	PRICE	QUANTITY	AMOUNT
72	*Vision Management©* Text - 144 pgs.	NEW!	DD1001	$ 24.95		
72	*Vision Management©* Text *If purchased at workshop*		DD1001W	$ 19.95		
72	*Challenging Students©* Text		DD1002	$ 19.95		
72	Pencil Holder		DD1003	$ 2.00		
72	*Intro to Vision Management©* Audio Tape		DD1004	$ 9.95		
72	Poster - Classroom Dedication (blue)		DD1005	$ 2.25		
72	Poster - Management Plan (yellow)	NEW!	DD1006	$ 2.25		
73	*Desktop Mentor©* Book	NEW!	DD1007B	$ 19.95		
73	*Every Day Answers©* - Easy access flip chart		DD1007F	$ 29.95		
73	*Day 2 Day©* Volume 1		DD1008	$ 29.95		
73	*Day 2 Day©* Volume 2		DD1009	$ 29.95		
74	*Goal For It! K-4©* (Includes two plush puppets)		DD1010	$ 19.95		
74	*Goal For It! 5-12©* (Advisory class, ISS book)	NEW!	DD1011	$ 16.95		
74	*VISIONS Character-Building Binder©*		DD1012	$249.95		
74	Imprinted Dividers for reproducible *VISIONS Binder©*		DD1013	$ 2.00		
75	*"911 for Parents"©* Video Training Kit (for training parents)		DD1014	$329.95		
75	*"911 for Parents"©* Video-Viewing Set (for lending to parents)		DD1015	$ 99.95		
76	*Enhance the Vision©* Text	NEW!	DD1019	$ 19.95		
available items that are not pictured catalog.	*Six-Point Plan for Raising Happy, Healthy Children*		DD1016	$ 8.95		
	Ending the Homework Hassle		DD1017	$ 9.95		
	My Personal Dictionary (for PK-3 students)		DD1018	$ 1.00		

SHIPPING & HANDLING (MINIMUM $5)		PRODUCT TOTAL	
ORDERS UNDER $250 ADD 10%		SHIPPING (MINIMUM $5.00)	
ORDERS OVER $250 ADD 9%		SUBTOTAL	
ORDERS OVER $1,000 ADD 8%		4% HAWAII TAX	
ORDERS OVER $5,000 ADD 6%		TOTAL	

Prices subject to change.
Please call to confirm before ordering.
4-20-04

School/District:_____ P.O. #_____

Name:_____ Day Phone:_____

Credit Card: __VISA __MASTERCARD

Address:_____

Credit Card #:_____

City:_____State_____Zip_____ Expiration Date:_____

DIANA DAY TRAINING PRODUCTS
discipline management made easy

2903 Saturn Road • Dept. EV04 • Garland, TX 75041
972-278-7773 • fax 972-278-8584
goals@dianaday.com • www.dianaday.com

PAGE #	ITEM		ITEM #	PRICE	QUANTITY	AMOUNT
72	*Vision Management* Text - 144 pgs.	NEW!	DD1001	$ 24.95		
72	*Vision Management* Text — If purchased at workshop		DD1001W	$ 19.95		
72	*Challenging Students* Text		DD1002	$ 19.95		
72	Pencil Holder		DD1003	$ 2.00		
72	*Intro to Vision Management* Audio Tape		DD1004	$ 9.95		
72	Poster - Classroom Dedication (blue)		DD1005	$ 2.25		
72	Poster - Management Plan (yellow)	NEW!	DD1006	$ 2.25		
73	*Desktop Mentor* Book	NEW!	DD1007B	$ 19.95		
73	*Every Day Answers* - Easy access flip chart		DD1007F	$ 29.95		
73	*Day 2 Day* Volume 1		DD1008	$ 29.95		
73	*Day 2 Day* Volume 2		DD1009	$ 29.95		
74	*Goal For It! K-4* (Includes two plush puppets)		DD1010	$ 19.95		
74	*Goal For It! 5-12* (Advisory class, ISS book)	NEW!	DD1011	$ 16.95		
74	*VISIONS Character-Building Binder*		DD1012	$249.95		
74	Imprinted Dividers for reproducible *VISIONS Binder*		DD1013	$ 2.00		
75	*"911 for Parents"* Video Training Kit (for training parents)		DD1014	$ 329.95		
75	*"911 for Parents"* Video-Viewing Set (for lending to parents)		DD1015	$ 99.95		
76	*Enhance the Vision* Text	NEW!	DD1019	$ 19.95		
Available items that are not pictured in catalog.	*Six-Point Plan for Raising Happy, Healthy Children*		DD1016	$ 8.95		
	Ending the Homework Hassle		DD1017	$ 9.95		
	My Personal Dictionary (for PK-3 students)		DD1018	$ 1.00		

SHIPPING & HANDLING (MINIMUM $5)

ORDERS UNDER $250 ADD 10%
ORDERS OVER $250 ADD 9%
ORDERS OVER $1,000 ADD 8%
ORDERS OVER $5,000 ADD 6%

Prices subject to change.
Please call to confirm before ordering.
4-20-04

PRODUCT TOTAL	
SHIPPING (MINIMUM $5.00)	
SUBTOTAL	
4% HAWAII TAX	
TOTAL	

School/District:_____ P.O. #_____

Name:_____ Day Phone:_____

Credit Card: __VISA __MASTERCARD

Address:_____

Credit Card #:_____

City:_____State_____Zip__   _____tion Date:_____